A Conversation with

Ernesto Mulato

A Conversation with

Ernesto Mulato

The Political and Military Struggle in Angola

Held on March 2, 1979
at the American Enterprise Institute for Public Policy Research
Washington, D.C.

ISBN 0–8447–3341–5

Library of Congress Catalog Card No. 79–53168

AEI Studies 238

Printed in the United States of America

Introduction

The media have a way of focusing a great deal of attention on a particular area and forgetting about the rest of the world. We are then rather surprised when major problems break out in an area that has been ignored. Ernesto Mulato is from a part of the world that has not received much media attention lately. He is a leader and member of the political bureau of UNITA (National Union for the Total Independence of Angola), a black nationalist movement in central and southern Angola.

It is generally agreed that if free elections were held in Angola, UNITA is the party that would win. Of course, no elections have been held and no elections are planned. Quite the contrary, military operations continue to escalate. In this conversation at the American Enterprise Institute, Mr. Mulato speaks about Angola's continuing political and military struggle and the growing Soviet-Cuban-Warsaw Pact presence in southern Africa.

JEANE J. KIRKPATRICK
Resident Scholar
American Enterprise Institute

A Conversation with Ernesto Mulato

I will try my best to convey the message of the Angolan people, under the leadership of Jonas Savimbi, who are engaged in a bitter struggle against Soviet expansion in Africa. Events of the past few weeks in Iran, Afghanistan, and Southeast Asia have occupied American attention more than the situation in my part of the world. However, we in UNITA feel we must share our experiences of the past three years.

Angola has become a vast cemetery and concentration camp. Our dream of free elections and independence has become a nightmare of foreign occupation. Our country, twice the size of Texas, has become an armed camp, a huge base used by the Soviets and the Cubans to arm and train others for takeovers in neighboring countries.

From our experience in Angola, we know the fate of neighboring Zaire, Zambia, and Namibia—if the Soviets and the Cubans are not resisted. It is a cruel fate that runs counter to everything an African nationalist cherishes—self-determination, independence, and security.

We hear the Katangese—black, Soviet-supported mercenaries—called progressives. We hear the West refer to the illegitimate government in Luanda as pragmatic, moderate, and nationalist. We hear the largest foreign expeditionary force in African history called a stabilizing factor in an era when the United States is heralding human rights. We hear from the West that the puppet government in Luanda would rather be aligned with the West but must allow foreign occupation forces to prevent invasion and to ensure Angola's independence. We hear that it is in the American interest to fund the Soviet-Cuban Vietnam by encouraging investment in Angola when the issue of who will govern our country is still undecided: 75 percent of the population refuses to live under Luanda's rule, UNITA controls more

3

than 50 percent of the country, and civil war is more widespread than at any time in the past three years. It sounds like the queen in *Alice in Wonderland* saying, "Prizes for everyone, everyone is a winner." Our former allies forget that the real losers in this game are those who share the West's belief in the right of the people to a democratic government. Andrew Young, your ambassador to the United Nations, has said that those who prefer to negotiate have no moral right to criticize those who engage in armed struggle.

UNITA has always preferred to negotiate. On five separate occasions, we encouraged all the Angolan parties to hammer out a compromise to prevent the tragedy of a civil war. We have always urged reconciliation and partnership among all Angolans in building the nation, but we have been prepared for armed struggle as well.

The American Declaration of Independence says that if a government cannot defend its citizens or create conditions of stability or provide material and spiritual well-being, the people have an obligation to overthrow it. We are used to fighting for freedom. We fought since 1966 against Portuguese colonialism and, since 1975, against Soviet and Cuban imperialism. We claim the moral right to resist a government that wants to force its will on our people with a brutal war machine run and funded by foreigners.

UNITA is used to going it alone unrecognized. I am sure our difficulties with the media are matched by the difficulties of the American people in finding out who we are. Much of this lack of information comes from the nature of our party and of our resistance. Since our beginning, we have fought from within Angola. We do not believe in having bases in other countries because we do not want to compromise our African brothers by our presence on their soil. Our future success must be determined by Angolans, not by good publicity. But we realize that this policy sometimes leaves our natural allies in the dark and fosters the current doubts and myths about the political realities facing southern Africa.

A good example of the misinformation about our struggle can be found in the *New York Times*. According to their maps, most of our support is in uninhabitable regions of the country. Maps depicting our military activities show our strength concentrated in areas similar to the Mojave Desert. Surely the editorial point of these graphics is to show some conspiratorial connection between us and South Africa. But, unfortunately, the region is inhabited by only a few snakes, lizards, cockroaches, and tumbleweed—men could last only twelve hours in the heat there—and we have no bone to pick with the lizards. We leave this area to the Cubans so they can enjoy

4

our wonderful climate. U.S. lack of information about our party dates back to the 1960s when Dr. Henry Kissinger prepared a paper on southern Africa for the National Security Council. He said we were the weakest group both militarily and politically. At that time we had 50 percent of the population behind us. Later, at the time of independence, polls showed UNITA with 65 to 75 percent support.

The ignorance of the West about our strength was understandable because the NATO countries had ties to Portugal, who never wanted to admit the degree of insurgence in Angola. Unfortunately, this intelligence vacuum has continued and could be very costly to the United States, which needs to maintain its credibility with the freedom fighters around the world.

The present web of totalitarian regimes is doomed to extinction. They have shown a total disregard for the welfare of their peoples, a total inability to address the crying needs of their countries, and a total lack of comprehension of the need to foster pluralistic societies. They are doomed because the will of the people can never be obliterated with troops, tanks, MiGs, or napalm. The United States must realize that the fight for freedom is a fight against Soviet totalitarianism. It is ironic that the United States did not discover UNITA until the U.S. government decided to aid the Angolan people in their attempt to prevent a Soviet takeover of our country.

The similarities between our beginnings are striking. Two hundred years ago, Americans fought a guerrilla struggle on native soil against the most powerful nation on earth. Today, we are doing the same. Americans advocated a democratic system and won. We are advocating the same, and we, too, will win and change the policies of southern Africa forever.

For the past three years, the Warsaw Pact nations have occupied our country and propped up the illegitimate government in Luanda. In those three years, more Angolans have died than in the entire war of liberation against the Portuguese. Thousands have been jailed or forcibly removed from their land and compelled to work under slavelike conditions away from their homes. Thousands more have been rounded up in trucks and shipped to Cuba to undergo indoctrination and cut sugar cane in the name of solidarity.

With Angola occupied by 26,500 soldiers, 8,000 Cuban civilian technicians, thousands of East Germans, Russians, and other Eastern Europeans, UNITA governs a territory containing over 3 million people—more than 50 percent of the population. In addition, 600,000 Angolans live in Zaire. In fact, 17 percent of the population of Kinshasa is Angolan. Another 20,000 are refugees in Zambia, and some 500,000 white Angolans live in Portugal, where they place a tremendous burden on the economy and exacerbate political tensions. Altogether, 75 percent of the population is not cooperating with the MPLA[1] rule. The rest are political prisoners, living under constant intimidation and physical abuse. That is the price we pay to remain Angolan.

In the abstract world of *realpolitik*, Soviet-Cuban occupation of one country might be dismissed as some strange quirk of fate. We do not have that luxury. Every day more Cubans come into the country. Since 1976, when Fidel Castro promised to withdraw 200 troops a week, Cuban troop strength has risen by one-third; civilian advisers by more than that. In December and January alone, an additional 1,800 Cubans arrived. They are bankrolled by the Soviets at a cost of $2.5 million a day. To date, the Soviet Union has spent nearly $2 billion on the war waged against us by the Cubans, the Warsaw Pact troops, and the Katangese. This also pays for the palace guard provided by the Cubans to prevent the numerous attempts to stage a coup by disillusioned army officers and members of Mr. Neto's party.

Our country is the base from which the Cubans, Russians, and East Germans have launched two invasions of Zaire in attempts to topple the government of Mobutu Sese Seko. They are now plotting the takeover of all of southern Africa. Angola has set the precedent for events in the Horn of Africa, Afghanistan, Iran, and the Middle East.

UNITA is able to speak frankly about the Soviets and Cubans because they have no leverage over us. Many of our African brothers are not so fortunate. During the day they must say a few words in support of the Soviets, but at night they eagerly discuss the day when the Soviets and Cubans will leave.

It is obvious that Africa does not want any foreign troops on its soil. Even in the face of a massive Soviet program of bribery and extortion, the 1976 meeting of the Organization of African Unity (OAU) in Addis Ababa voted 22 to 22 to condemn the Soviet presence —quite a show of courage considering that Cuban troops and advisers were stationed in nineteen countries.

In 1975 President Kenneth Kaunda of Zambia warned the world that Russia was a tiger trying to get in the back door. Today, the tiger is in.

Africans do not want the Soviet-Cuban military presence, but

---

[1] Popular Movement for the Liberation of Angola, which has Soviet-Cuban support.

they have no choice. They found little desire on the part of the West to resist expansionism, this new imperialism. To preserve what autonomy they have left, the governments in the region "play ball" with the Soviets. They know from history that they must accommodate the Soviets if they are to stay in power and not be replaced by a more vicious, less humanistic government.

Many Americans in positions of power cavalierly dismiss the Soviet dreams of empire as the normal prerogative of a superpower to control a set of client states. The history of African nationalism should be a lesson to these people. We have fought long and hard to make the point that there can be no return to nineteenth-century imperialism.

Western analysts attempting to understand this new imperialism have theorized about the common ties that bind Africans to Cubans— a history of struggle, resistance, and oppression. According to some, Castro has become a modern David, but David never fought on the side of Goliath. Castro is said to be the new messiah of Africa, selflessly working alongside the common people to help them become free. But it is sheer nonsense to believe that the Cubans are in Angola out of love for my countrymen. The Cuban soldier is not a Peace Corps worker. Behind the smokescreen of talk about solidarity, liberation, progressiveness, and democracy, lie agents of death and chaos. Were Cuban pilots so excited by the revolutionary romance of Angola that they pleaded with the Soviets to guard Cuban air space until they came back?

While the Western media is taken in by the utterances of Castro, columns of coffins wait for burial outside Luanda cemeteries. In Cuba, honor guards watch as empty caskets are placed in the ground. The bodies are left on the battlefield to rot. The families are told that their sons died by accident in Angola. We are the accident, the Angolan people.

Many in the West have come to believe that the young soldiers volunteer to serve in Angola out of ideological concern. Instead, they are the unemployed and the peasants from the poorest sections of Cuba, eager for a chance to own a house or estate in Angola. It is an ingenious solution to domestic unrest and economic problems. Ship the problem to Angola.

Castro's interest in the Angolan venture is obvious: at the time of the Soviet-Cuban invasion, his star was fading. Tito of Yugoslavia, the leader of the nonaligned movement, was disturbing the Soviets by his increasing criticism and his overtures to the West. Castro's previous liberation adventures had failed miserably and his economy was shattered. What better way to get back in the limelight than by having Moscow sponsor his claim to leadership of the Third World? As a result, the nonaligned movement faces the prospect of being subverted by the Soviets. We cannot encourage the Cubans to place troops in another nineteen African countries. They are nothing but proxies and marionettes of the Russians.

The Soviet-Cuban presence in Angola is not just an internal African problem but an international one. I think the American public understands this, but I am not so sure about certain analysts and experts. Without their initial victory in Angola, during the days of the conventional fighting, would the Cubans and Soviets have dared to invade the Horn? Absolutely not.

The Russian presence in Angola and Ethiopia is of strategic importance to the West. Both countries lie on, or near, vital oil shipping routes. Angola, which is rich in oil, has vast reserves of strategic minerals. It is the gateway to Zaire and Zambia, other countries with minerals vital to Western economies and defense systems. South of us lies Namibia and South Africa, which are also rich in resources.

The entire industrialized free world depends on southern Africa for crucial materials used in defense and in advanced technology. Approximately one-third of the minerals and metals imported by the United States comes from this area. For Europe, the percentage is much higher. To think that your technological expertise will win over Soviet armaments is to be naive.

At the very least, the cost of these minerals and oil will increase dramatically because of the Soviet presence. The terms of business will fluctuate with the ideological mood and opportunism of the government. Access to minerals will be restricted because of widespread conflict, and transportation lines will continue to be beyond repair or so congested as to be impracticable. The situation will be perpetually unstable, but the Soviets will remain in control of the capitals. What is happening in Africa now will affect Europe dramatically in the next few years and will negatively alter the balance of power in the world.

Soviet ineptitude in Africa in the 1960s lulled many to believe that Africans have a natural antipathy to the Soviets. Ambassador Young has even claimed that because Africans are religious, we can never be dominated by Communists. No, it is because of our religion that we can endure years of persecution and oppression. Maybe, if the situation continues, we will produce a pope.

In the 1960s the Soviets did not use proxies, they did not use the largest expeditionary force in African history, they did not make extensive use of the East German Afrika Corps—and they were not successful in playing the power broker. Apparently they have learned from their mistakes. Without any resistance against the newest Cecil Rhodes, it is unrealistic to hope that the Soviet presence in Africa is transitory.

The Soviet desire to recolonize Africa is based on a global strategy aimed at intensifying rivalry in the West over increasingly diminishing sources of raw materials. After the fall of Indochina, the Soviets foresaw a transfer of European investment to Africa. They noted fifteen years of trade deficits between Europe and Africa, and they projected greater deficits in the 1970s and 1980s as demand for strategic metals and petroleum products increased.

The April 1974 coup in Portugal afforded the Soviets the opportunity to implement their policy for southern Africa. They forced the United States into the reactive stance of trying to walk a tightrope between the heavily American-financed economies of white rule in southern Africa and black Africa.

Since putting Agostinho Neto in power, they have confronted the United States in Zaire, Namibia, and Zimbabwe and are challenging American investment policies in South Africa. They want to strike at the vulnerable economies of Western Europe and force them into accommodation, thus depriving the United States of any means to counter Soviet influence.

Despite the opinion of many experts, Angola was not an unlikely spot for a superpower confrontation. In 1973 and 1974 our country had the best transportation system, the best harbor facilities, and one of the healthiest economies in southern Africa. The Benguela Railway was vital to Zaire and Zambia. Iron ore, gold, diamonds, manganese, uranium, and oil were found in great quantities although 75 percent of Angola's territory has never been systematically surveyed for other mineral deposits. We were one of the few countries in Africa to export food and one of the largest coffee producers in the world. Above all, we were in a strategic position along the shipping routes of the South Atlantic. In 1975 my country was a nice plum for the new adventurers.

The Soviets had two goals after the coup in Portugal. First, they wanted to put the Moscow-oriented Portuguese Communist party in power in Lisbon. They almost succeeded by immediately seizing control of Portugal's unions, media, and armed forces. Second, they wanted to put the Portuguese Communist party's longtime ally, the MPLA, in power in Luanda. However, the Alvor Agreement between the three Angolan parties and the Portuguese government rigorously stipulated the mechanics of a free election and establishment of democratic institutions. When Savimbi landed in Luanda to cheering throngs of over a half million people, it was obvious who would win the election. The superpowers had supposed that Neto had his strongest support in the capital, but he was greeted by less than 100,000 people.

UNITA rallies drew crowds of more than a million. Independent observers estimated we had 65 to 75 percent of the support while the FNLA[2] and the MPLA split the rest. Yet, we believed that Angola should be ruled by a democratic government composed of all three parties. We constantly tried to avoid civil war by bringing the parties together to reach an agreement. The Soviets and the MPLA, as the weakest party, did not want elections, however, and conspired with the radical element in the Portuguese armed forces to cancel unilaterally the provisions of the Alvor Agreement. Close to three-quarters of the MPLA army had deserted because of Neto's alignment with Moscow, so outside troops were needed to put him in power and deprive Savimbi of the presidency. Cuba was the logical choice.

Much of the testimony before congressional committees has stated that the Cubans entered the fight because of the South African invasion. But where are the South African troops in Angola now? If the Cubans are there to guard against South African invaders, why did they do nothing when South Africa attacked the SWAPO[3] bases in Cassinga last May? Why have the Cubans escalated their troop strength when South Africans are no longer in Angola?

Soviet arms were being delivered to Angolan ports and cities long before other powers became involved. UNITA supporters in the dockworkers' union went on strike during the transitional government: they refused to unload ships containing Soviet armaments destined for the MPLA and the Portuguese. Cubans appeared in southern areas of Angola in March 1975, nearly seven months before the South African invasion. Many American and Canadian missionaries who were later evacuated saw them in remote towns and villages.

Now American experts propagate the Cuban version of the event, and history is being revised to put freedom, independence, justice, and self-determination on the side of those very people who pervert those ideals. UNITA resistance against the Soviets and the Cubans

---

[2] An insurgent party in northern Angola.

[3] South West Africa People's Organization.

has fallen on deaf ears. The United States is haunted by the specter of Vietnam.

Some suggest that the Soviets are now involved in their own Vietnam. It is true. UNITA is costing them $2.5 million a day. We have killed nearly 8,000 Cuban soldiers. The Portuguese, with three times as many troops, could not control Angola, and there is no reason to believe that the Cubans can. History is on our side. But the longer the war is protracted, the more our people suffer morally and physically. By sitting on its hands, the West encourages the next moves by the Soviets, which will be devastating not only to southern Africa but to the West as well.

Angola is now an armed camp. The so-called pragmatic regime of Neto has created concentration camps at São Nicolau, outside Moçâmedes, and near Saurimo in the Lunda district. There are prisons in Luanda, Huambo, Luso, and Sá da Bandeira, containing thousands of political prisoners. These prisoners include the nationalist element of MPLA, former party officials and army officers, Jehovah's Witnesses, followers of the religious leader Simon Toco, FNLA and UNITA sympathizers, and Catholic and Protestant clergy. Recently, when UNITA took over a government prison near Serpa Pinto, it released 800 prisoners who had been living in subhuman conditions and subjected to torture.

What other people call solidarity, we call slavery. The Angolan people are not being fooled. Our ancestors were taken into slavery and our country virtually depopulated. Then we were forced to work on the cocoa plantations in São Tomé and, later, we were taken from our lands to work under the hated system of contract labor. Today, people view the actions of the government as equally unjust.

The government has embarked on a massive program of relocation, not for economic but for political reasons. It wants to destroy all resistance by destroying Angolan culture and by separating families. It rewards loyal party members with large tracts of our villagers' land.

The United States has condemned the South African passbook system which prohibits the free movement of blacks within the country. For many years, the Portuguese had a similar system, but they dropped the practice because it was so deeply hated. But now, Angolans have revived the use of identification cards and foist them on their fellow countrymen.

The MPLA, which has a twenty-year friendship treaty with the Soviet Union, calls itself the workers' party, which is ridiculous because 90 percent of our people are farmers. In the name of the

11

Angolan worker they have adopted a draconian work code. Anyone late for work, works the next three days without pay. Anyone slow on the job, goes to jail. No matter how unsafe the working conditions or how meager the wages, a protest to the factory management means two years in prison.

These policies are hardly winning the support of the people. Plagued by food shortages and massive unemployment, the workers are ignoring MPLA appeals in the name of the proletariat. They are staging slowdowns and wildcat strikes at the main ports of Lobito and Luanda. The rash of industrial sabotage indicates what the workers think about the workers' party.

An example of this refusal to work under the Soviets and the Cubans is the flight of nearly 16,000 laborers, or 80 percent of the work force, from the diamond mines in Lunda province. As a result, diamonds, once 10 percent of our exports, are now mined on a small scale. This situation might also account for the nationalization of Diamang.

Neto has had every church, mission school, and hospital in central Angola destroyed or closed. The government has made no attempt to replace the vital health and educational services provided by these institutions to over 400,000 people. Those connected with churches have lost everything: all Protestant and Catholic property has been confiscated and all clergy either banished or imprisoned. Clergy in the central areas of Angola live in UNITA camps to avoid persecution. There they continue their vital educational and medical functions.

The Baptist churches in northern Angola have been razed, and an estimated 200,000 Baptists have fled to Zaire. Ambassador Young might be interested in the destruction of the Hualondo mission in southern Angola, founded by black Americans over fifty years ago. It was the mission he was to be assigned to before he became a politician. It lies in ruins.

Neto's recent overtures to the West have encouraged some to regard the MPLA more favorably. Suddenly it is being called the party most qualified to govern Angola. UNITA believes that the Angolan people are the best judges of which party is best qualified.

The present government is unable to make the economy work. Before the civil war, Angola had a healthy growth rate of 11 to 14 percent, and Western economists project the same rate for this year. But is this possible when a half million Portuguese technicians, merchants, and ranchers are gone? Is this possible when the elaborate network of roads built before the civil war to link our domestic market is unusable because of UNITA's military activities?

The once prosperous coffee *fazendas* in the north have been burned by their owners to protest the Soviet-Cuban occupation. Angola must import 80 percent of its food. The mines are shut down, and the vast Cunene Hydroelectric Project has not worked for four years. Almost all government revenues from Gulf Oil royalties, which account for 90 percent of Angola's money, goes to food because UNITA controls 85 percent of Angola's arable land. The breadbasket of Angola, the central highlands, has always produced all of Angola's meat and wheat and is a UNITA stronghold. As a result, there is no food in the cities.

Perhaps the most dramatic symbol of the government's paralysis and the Cubans' inability to crush our resistance is the Benguela Railway. It does not work. In many areas it no longer exists, because we have taken the rails and ties into the bush with us. Yet, every two months, like clockwork, Neto announces that the Benguela is opening and that traffic between Angola and Zaire is about to resume. The announcement is dutifully printed in the Western press as a sign that he is finally in control, but nothing happens. At his much publicized reconciliation with Zaire, Neto promised to open the Benguela, but he knew he could not because it runs through the central, eastern, and southern areas of the country that we control.

Many times in the past three years Cuban, East German, and Katangese mercenaries have swept through the region to clear the route, but they have always failed. At present, UNITA attacks the railway about four times a week. In areas where the railway has been repaired, we destroy the locomotives built by General Electric. We are using the same methods against the Moçâmedes Railway, which extends to the mountain of iron in Cassinga. In addition, much of the early support for Dr. Savimbi came from Angolan railway workers, and UNITA still retains their loyalty. Thus, the working of the railroad depends on UNITA. There can never be enough foreign technicians in Angola to run the Benguela and keep it in repair, and locomotive replacement lags far behind the frequency of our military operations.

As Luanda tries to lure the United States into business relations it might be wise to recognize how little power the government has. Besides UNITA territory, it does not have effective control over Malange, Cuanza Norte, which is the strategic entrance to Luanda, or even Luanda itself. The Portuguese weekly, the *Nation*, for January 5, 1979, reported increased UNITA activity in the capital. Every morning, people wake up to find the walls painted with UNITA flags. Cubans, FAPLA (Luanda's armed forces), and MPLA officials cannot go to the *musseques,* our shanty towns where most of the population lives, because they would be killed.

The people resent the Cubans not only because they are aggressors and colonialists, but also because they have become a great burden. The homes and plantations of the Portuguese have gone to the Cubans and their families, particularly the former *colonatos* around Cela and the Caconda. Angolans have no houses. There is little food, and what is available goes first to the Cubans. The country's revenue is used to pay the Cuban civilians. Angolans come second. The Cuban presence has created an astronomical rate of inflation, making Angolans virtually unable to buy goods and food on the rare occasions they are available.

The elevation of the Cuban to colonial master is even blunter on the battlefield, where the Cubans have combat rations, but the FAPLA troops must forage for their meals. After battles, we have seen helicopters take dead Cubans to town for burial, while wounded FAPLA troops are left on the ground to die. All strategy and commands are dictated by the Cubans and Soviets, spreading deep resentment within the MPLA ranks. The result has been increased desertions and coup attempts.

Not only does the Luanda regime have little power internally, but it also cannot control Katangese and Soviet use of Angola as a base for subversion against neighboring countries. The idea that the West should deal with Luanda so that peaceful solutions can be found for the region is madness. Neto can profess his desire for better relations with the West and promise to control the Katangese and facilitate a peaceful solution to Namibia, but he has no control over any of these things. He is no Anwar Sadat; he cannot turn around tomorrow and tell the Soviets to leave.

In the first stage of the civil war, Neto and the FAPLA officers worked with the Katangese against us. The 13,000 Katangese soldiers are in Angola fighting for pay, not beliefs. Their allegiance is to no one, not even to their beloved Shaba (formerly Katanga) province in Zaire. They have been fighting against us from the beginning, first for the Portuguese counterinsurgency forces and now for the Soviets and the Cubans. They are the same soldiers who fought for Moise Tshombe in his secessionist bid, and now Moscow calls them the liberators of Zaire. How they would act after such a liberation has never been discussed. We in Angola know them to be the most ruthless and savage of fighters who rape our women, massacre villagers,

14

and plunder wherever they go. The Cubans use them for search and destroy missions since the Cubans and MPLA no longer come into the bush after us.

After the conventional fighting in 1976, the Katangese mercenaries were rewarded with their own bases and camps in Lunda province. Later they were put under the command of the Cubans and, most recently, the East Germans. The Katangese are essentially a black Soviet foreign legion. Both invasions of Shaba were supported by the Russians in the form of technical training and massive arms supplies. The Cubans provided training at Boma, a former Protestant mission near Luso in Moxico province, at Chimbilia and Camissombo in Lunda province, and at Catumbela, east of Lobito in Benguela province. The East Germans conducted the strategy on the battlefield. Today, steady infiltration into Zaire's Shaba province makes it more vulnerable to Katangese takeover than ever before.

Any promises by Neto to control the Katangese and to monitor the long border between Zaire and Angola are untenable. The job is similar to U.S. attempts to prevent illegal Mexican immigrants from entering this country.

The Soviets are continuing massive arms shipments into Angola, and there are more Russians in the country than at the beginning of the civil war. They manage the Angolan ports of Barra do Cuanza, south of Luanda, and Porto Alexandre, south of Moçâmedes, to expedite the unloading of ever-increasing quantities of sophisticated weaponry. High-ranking Soviet army officials are taking a more direct hand in training liberation groups at various camps around the country. In addition to plotting MPLA strategy, they are now participating in logistical operations in the combat zones.

Near Moçâmedes, the Soviets have constructed one of the largest military airfields on the continent. The size of the installation indicates its purpose—the rapid mobilization and airlifting of troops to other countries. Neto attended the ribbon-cutting ceremonies and named the airport after our national hero, the astronaut, Yuri Gagarin. To the Angolan people, this is as insulting as naming our towns after Salazar. Also near Moçâmedes, the Soviets have been planning for the past two years to erect a vast radio complex to monitor Namibia, South Africa, and the South Atlantic shipping lanes. So far, our military operations have made this venture impossible.

From our experience fighting the Soviet-Cuban occupation, UNITA has concluded that, if the Cubans are not thrown out of Angola within two or three years, the situation in central and southern Africa will dramatically change in favor of the Soviet Union. If the

Soviets are allowed to expand their sphere of influence unchecked, the West will lose an effective voice in the region. But there is still time. UNITA has conducted a very vigorous resistance.

After the cities fell in February 1976, UNITA was crushed. The people were demoralized to see their hopes for independence smashed by the tanks and the MiGs the Soviets and Cubans threw at us. There was considerable debate about our next move.

Savimbi walked the length and the breadth of the countryside canvassing the people about whether to continue the resistance. In areas far from the Cubans these meetings sometimes numbered in the hundreds of thousands. Some were small gatherings at remote villages; others were held on the outskirts of Cuban-occupied cities. The people agreed that our cause was just and that we had to continue.

Dr. Savimbi vowed to stay in the bush and fight. The next few months we reorganized our army and visited base camps to attend to the pressing problems of hundreds of refugees, who had evacuated the cities. Then we started fighting back.

Today, UNITA controls virtually all of five provinces—Moxico, Bié, Cuando-Cubango, Huambo, and Cunene. We are gaining the upper hand against the Cubans, East Germans and FAPLA in the six others—Benguela, Moçâmedes, Cuanza Sul, Cuanza Norte, Malange, and Lunda. UNITA is more powerful, politically and materially, than at any time in its history. In the past two years we have progressed from a guerilla war to semiregular fighting. We have more trained soldiers and arms than ever and are politically active in every region of the country and among every class and ethnic group. We have the arms, the soldiers, the people, and the land to win.

At first, we concentrated on cutting transportation and communication lines between Cuban garrisons, ambushing military convoys, sabotaging the railway, and encircling the cities. Now, we are moving to take and hold small and medium-sized towns. In many regions we have forced Cubans into wholesale withdrawal. We can infiltrate the cities at will.

The people have supported us. The Cuban force, demoralized and weakened, has retreated to garrisons to protect Soviet economic interests, knowing they cannot subjugate the population, but this is small consolation to us when Angola has become a gulag.

If America reasserts its leadership in the world, we can accelerate the defeat of the Soviets and the Cubans, but if it does not, the struggle will be protracted, our society and culture will be further shattered, and our prospects for building a democratic society dimmer.

Asking the United States to reassert its leadership role is not a veiled request for troops, advisers, or arms. We do not need that type of help. We ask Americans to remember their revolutionary beginnings, which inspire us. We ask the United States to use diplomatic means to facilitate a solution to our country's occupation.

UNITA under Savimbi has consistently advocated national unity, peace, and free elections. We have never claimed the exclusive right to govern Angola. We are the most popular party, but we are also the most persistent defenders of Angolan freedom and nationalism. No matter when elections are held, we will win, but the legacy of the civil wars in Zaire, Sudan, and Nigeria has taught us that to outlaw, suppress, or exclude the other two parties would not benefit us or Angola. The only way to stabilize the entire region is to sponsor a government of national unity. That is *realpolitik*. Not until then will the problem of Namibia be solved, the threat to Zaire cease, or a solution to Zimbabwe be found. The West has been eager to offer initiatives on Zimbabwe and Namibia, but not on Angola, which set the precedent.

UNITA believes the burning issues in southern Africa can be solved only by African dialogue and by elections free from foreign intervention. We dream of an independent region devoted to cooperation in development and nation-building.

The U.S. attitude toward the Soviet-Cuban occupation baffles us. The pattern of Soviet expansionism in Africa is clear. How can we reconcile the justification of the Cubans as a stabilizing influence by some Americans with American defense of human rights?

The United States calls for human rights in Russia, Cuba, and Europe but accepts Cubans in Angola killing our people. There is no possibility of human rights in a country where a minority group was put in power by a great expeditionary force. There are no human rights in a country where everyone is a political prisoner.

We will never accept a peace that means capitulation to the new colonialists or living in fear. We will never accept a peace that destroys our Angolan identity for some alien ideology. Imagine our reaction when we hear that the United States is to enter into relations with Luanda to protect U.S. economic interests. The Gulf Oil installation is helping maintain the Soviet-Cuban presence. Angolans do not benefit from American business interests, which employ few Angolans.

U.S. corporations in Africa have not been democratic or concerned with human rights. They are pursuing an illusory short-term interest. When our country is free and stable, we will need their help to rebuild it. By engaging in a policy conceived for the short run, they jeopardize long-term interests not only in Angola but in all of southern Africa. The desire of Boeing, Texaco, Citibank, Gulf, and others to negotiate with Luanda is a serious mistake. The safety of their employees cannot be assured, and the country's instability makes their investments risky. With escalation in the fighting, conditions for conducting business will rapidly deteriorate, especially in the major cities, and the recent installation of more Soviet-oriented personnel in the MPLA cabinet will add to the difficulty of doing business.

Recently, the Arthur D. Little Company of Cambridge, Massachusetts, became a consultant to the Luanda regime. Their report, mimicking the Hudson Institute report of the late 1960s, called for massive development of Angola's coast and encouragement of American investment. Both reports, the latter made to the Portuguese, said that investment was safe along the coast away from the battle zones. This is foolishness.

Our military activities run south of Luanda to the Cunene River and cover territory where such development would take place. Transportation systems in these areas are not functional. Americans will have to be brought in by air, a risky business, and escorted by armed guard. More American investment in Angola will merely give the Soviets a rationale for increasing their troop presence, since anything having to do with the economy must be secured against the people's resistance.

American corporations should realize they cannot do business with an illegitimate government under foreign occupation. The situation is not comparable to that of Taiwan and the People's Republic of China. We have been in control of most of Angola since 1976 and have been the majority party for longer. It pains us to see the United States consider granting legitimacy to the morally reprehensible. How can it condemn the Katangese who threaten American interests in Zaire and condone those who support the Katangese and supply them with arms?

At one time, we were allies against the biggest war machine Africa had ever seen. We understand that the U.S. government was paralyzed by Watergate and the investigations of the Central Intelligence Agency (CIA) when it cut off support to us. We went our own way because we believe in self-sufficiency. But at least the United States had the moral courage to press for Cuban withdrawal and a peaceful solution to our civil war. Today, we ask the U.S. government to look at the pattern of Soviet expansionism and respond to it. We urge it to withhold recognition of Angola and to press for an end to our civil war and an end to Cuban occupation.

As for us, our resistance is absolute. With the support of the Angolan people, UNITA will triumph.

Questions and Answers

Scott Sullivan, American Federation of Government Employees: Does UNITA enjoy a good relationship with other African liberation organizations, such as SWAPO in Namibia and the ELF and the ETLF in Eritrea?

Mr. Mulato: We previously had cordial relations with SWAPO because UNITA helped SWAPO infiltrate into Namibia. When we were fighting the Portuguese, it was difficult for SWAPO to continue their struggle because they had no areas from which to operate. Our party gave them bases from which they could infiltrate into their country.

SWAPO has always depended on outside support for money and supplies. We understood that they needed the support of the Soviet Union to survive and we could still permit them to come into Angola because they were fighting a just cause. After the coup d'etat in Portugal and UNITA's retreat into the bush, however, we had no way to maintain contact, and SWAPO was forced to work with the MPLA. Since they are now working with MPLA, we do not have relations with them.

After the retreat we were also cut off from contact with the other liberation movements. Now we are trying to get in touch with other movements fighting a just cause, like the one in Eritrea.

Tomin Weashan, Voice of America: I am from Mozambique, where under the colonial system we were educated to respect whites and mulattoes. But when independence came the government could make the handling of whites and mulattoes an issue of confrontation with the opposition party.

The government in Luanda claims it is more multiracial than UNITA because it includes not only mulattoes but also white ministers. Dr. Savimbi seems to defend the ideology of negritude, which means Angola is going to be mostly for black Africans. How do the two parties really stand on the issue?

Mr. Mulato: I think the proportion of whites in each party was an accident of history. UNITA was founded in 1966 because of the failure of the two liberation movements. Those involved in its forma-

19

tion were young students, and the majority were blacks, but that does not mean that we do not have mulattoes.

I think your question, however, is whether we have white members. We do have whites in our party.

When the coup d'etat took place in Portugal, UNITA realized it was time to negotiate, so we agreed to a cease-fire with the Portuguese government. Because we initiated the cease-fire the MPLA later claimed we were a creature of the Portuguese and favored white people.

The Alvor Agreement shows that the MPLA and FNLA refused citizenship to the whites born in Angola. UNITA was the only party that defended the right of the Portuguese born in Angola to become Angolan citizens if they desired. President Savimbi challenged the idea that a mulatto citizen of Angola could have the right to refuse his father citizenship through an accident of color.

We are not racists, and UNITA does not believe that any country should be mainly for blacks or mainly for whites.

In the bush white people are commanding some of our forces, and mulattoes are fighting beside us. They refuse to live with the Cubans because they reject their system and the minority government of Luanda.

ERNEST LEFEVER, Ethics and Public Policy Center of Georgetown University: I have a question about the military situation in Angola at the time the U.S. Senate refused to give UNITA the $30 million requested by the administration. At that time, UNITA was supported by South African forces. How close were you to taking Luanda?

MR. MULATO: The South Africans became involved in Angola because of the Cuban presence. Although our forces were advancing, we never expected them to put us in power. We knew that if UNITA obtained control through South African intervention the people would resent them the same way they resent the Cubans today. What we were pressing for was a reconciliation so we could agree on elections. We never expected to take Luanda by force with South African aid.

ROBERT WOODSON, American Enterprise Institute: Does UNITA continue to receive aid from South Africa?

MR. MULATO: Since retreating into the bush, we have had no help from South Africa, although we still use weapons left by their forces involved in the civil war.

In 1977 Dr. Savimbi left Angola to seek aid, which is why Neto was suddenly eager to restore relations with Zaire. Dr. Savimbi was able to get some assistance from friendly countries, and we now have supplies flown in. As I said, Angola is big and difficult to control, especially without the support of the people, so we can fly in supplies at any time. But, to repeat, we have no support from South Africa anymore.

MR. WOODSON: What would be the impact of Namibian independence on the future of UNITA?

MR. MULATO: I don't think there will be any impact. When we fought against the Portuguese, no border country gave us assistance. We mainly fought inside the country with the people and, at the end of the war with the Portuguese, we were the only party whose leadership was inside Angola. The MPLA, which was thought to be the most powerful party, did not have sufficient guerilla strength, which is why the Katangese were recruited.

We would welcome independence for Namibia, but we must concentrate on our struggle for the liberation of Angola.

ANGELO CORDOVILLA, U.S. Senate staff: There has been a great deal of talk in the United States about what role the CIA might have played in Angola in 1975. Many different things have been said, and it is difficult to tell where the truth lies. Could you say if the people there were of any help to you or if they actually got in your way?

MR MULATO: When we fought the Portuguese, as I said, we never had support from the outside. After the coup, many countries became aware that we had the support of the people but that we needed aid.

In less than three months, almost all African states, including Tanzania and the Congo Republic, gave us assistance. All outside assistance was from the African states, and we did not ask where they got it. Our only concern was to get assistance. We did not have any deal that the CIA was advising, and the people involved never admitted working for the CIA.

PENN KEMBLE, Senator Patrick Moynihan's staff: How would you characterize current U.S. policy toward the Neto government and toward UNITA? And what changes would you suggest the administration make in these policies? Also, does UNITA have any contacts in the State Department?

MR. MULATO: First, UNITA has no contacts with the State Department. Second, we do not expect any assistance from the United States, either in arms or troops. But, as a peace-loving country, the United States could use diplomatic means to press for Cuban and Soviet withdrawal. It could apply diplomatic pressure directly on the Luanda regime, through friendly countries that have diplomatic relations with Luanda, or on Cuba directly. This is the least the administration could do because the Cubans went to Angola when they found that the United States was no longer interested in defending democratic institutions there. It would not be necessary to send marines to Angola—that would be refused—but a declaration that no foreign troops should be involved in Angola could change the pattern.

As for policy toward the Luanda regime, lobbying for its recognition is increasing. Such an action would be a mistake for the United States because it still has a moral obligation to defend democratic institutions. Our struggle is different from that of Vietnam because we are the majority in Angola. Being the majority, we should be involved in building our country.

MIKE SAMUELS, Georgetown Center for Strategic and International Studies: I am confused. You suggest that UNITA would like diplomatic support from the United States. UNITA claims an interest not in taking over the country, but in a coalition government in which it would have a part. And it would also like the United States to exert influence on European countries that have relations with Angola in an effort to get a Cuban withdrawal.

Given UNITA's goals, wouldn't it be preferable for the United States to have relations with the Angolan government and deal directly with it on your behalf?

MR. MULATO: Although I said we do not expect to take over Angola with the help of mercenaries, like South Africans, I did not say that we do not expect to take over. In fighting a war, the objective is to take power.

On the other hand, U.S. recognition of the Luanda regime would not defend Angolan interests so long as the Cubans are in the country. U.S. recognition with the Cubans there would only help the Soviet Union whose policies the Cubans are defending. Putting money in Angola is not going to soften Neto; it is going to pay for the Soviets to invade Zaire.

UNITA has been accused of changing its policy because the MPLA wants relations with the West. We have not changed. We are maintaining our ideological line, but we still want coexistence.

Even if the United States recognizes Luanda, the only real effect will be to prolong the war because the majority of the population is ready to die rather than to live under the colonialism of the Cubans. The burden will fall on the Angolan people and on Africa in general.

Q: In most extended analyses of the situation in Angola, Dr. Savimbi is said to be UNITA, implying there is no other leadership in the party. Therefore, countries that might support UNITA fear that if something should happen to Savimbi, UNITA would disintegrate. Would you care to comment?

MR. MULATO: We are aware of this impression, but it is not true because UNITA has a collective leadership. Those who think Dr. Savimbi is the main threat to the Luanda government are mistaken, because if something happens to him the situation is going to polarize even more. He is a moderating influence. Some people do not want to make any compromises with the MPLA. They feel we have suffered enough and should fight for total power.

Without Dr. Savimbi the war would continue, but its goals might be very different. We pray that he stays until the end of our struggle.

DATE DUE